COPYRIGHT

Charisse Resser

Easy Family Meals Even Your Toddler Will Eat © 2015, Charisse Resser

Easy Toddler Meals

easytoddlermeals@gmail.com

ALL RIGHTS RESERVED.

This book contains material protected under International and Federal Copyright Laws and Treaties. Any unauthorized reprint or use of this material is prohibited. No part of this book may be reproduced or transmitted in any form or by any means, electronic or mechanical, including photocopying, recording, or by any information storage and retrieval system without express written permission from the author.

www.easytoddlermeals.com

All photos are property of Easy Toddler Meals

DISCLAIMER
All content presented in this book is for informational purposes only. These statements have not been evaluated by the Food and Drug Administration. This product is not intended to diagnose, treat, cure or prevent any disease, nor is it intended to be a substitute for medical treatment. Please seek the advice of your healthcare professional for your specific health concerns.

TABLE OF CONTENTS

About The Author 4
Introduction 5

Breakfast

Carrot Eggless Pancakes 6
Egg Toast Cups 8
Blueberry Bites 10
Cheese Spinach Muffins 12
The Patterned Sandwiches 14
Breakfast Bites To-Go 16
Quinoa Oatmeal 18
Strawberry Cream Cheese Rollups 20

Lunch

Pizza Bites 22
Blooming Spinach 24
Kale Pasta Salad 26
Broccoli Cheese Roll-Ups 28
Tuna Cranberry Almond Salad Sandwich Circles 30
Stuffed French Toast 32
Cauliflower Mozzarella Sticks 34

Dinner

Macadamia Crusted Cod With Mango Salsa 36
Creamy Mushroom Chicken 38
Sweet And Sour Chicken Meatballs 40
Slow Cooker Beef And Broccoli 42
Bell Pepper Beef Steak 44
Baked Chicken Parmesan With "Noodles" 46
Chili Cornbread Muffins 48
One Pan Chicken Tenders With Asparagus 50

Dessert

Frozen Bananas 52
Green Chocolate Chip Cookies 54
Cinammon Toast Sticks 56
French Toast Sticks 58
Banana Walnut Ice Cream With Buttery Bananas 60
Apple Chocolate Chips 62
Zero Sugar Banana Walnut Mini Loaves 64
Veggie "Cupcakes" With Greek Yogurt Frosting 66

ABOUT THE AUTHOR

When Charisse Resser realized her son ate just about anything, she decided it was time to start cooking. Charisse knows firsthand that parents have a small window of time to figure out what to cook for the kids, and an even smaller window of time with which to cook it in. She began posting pictures of her quick and easy creations on social media sites like Instagram and Facebook so she could share them with her friends and family. The accounts flourished and are now followed by thousands of moms and dads from around the world. She is well known for her quick snapshot 10-15 second recipe videos. And she's even been known to make carrots walk and bell peppers dance; how's that for talent?

Charisse is an Emmy nominated television journalist, who reported for ABC, CBS, and CNN affiliates. She graduated magna cum laude from the University of Southern California. Charisse is now an entrepreneur in the field of healthcare education. Cooking is her hobby, and seeing her family enjoy her meals brings her great joy.

INTRODUCTION

Thank you for purchasing my book. After showcasing my recipes on social media, I'm thrilled to share them in a published form. In this book, you will find a collection of my recipes including pictures and short videos. You can access the videos either on my Instagram profile page or by using a Quick Response Code Reader (QR) app on your phone or tablet.

I hope this book inspires you to cook for your whole family, and of course your 3 foot tall little love bug or bugs! The recipes are easy, delicious, and simple.

A huge thank you for your support. I hope you enjoy these recipes as much as my family does!

You can also go to my website at www.easytoddlermeals.com for more recipes. The site has an easy search function and also a recipe index for you to look for dishes to make.

Cheers to Eating,
Charisse

 www.facebook.com/easytoddlermeal

 @easytoddlermeals

DEDICATION

I dedicate this book to my two boys, my son and husband. They're the real reason I cook. I'm not sure where it all goes, but my toddler son eats like a teenage boy. Obviously, he takes after his foodie mom. Enjoy and cheers to eating!

 www.youtube.com/easytoddlermeals

 @easytoddlermeal

 www.pinterest.com/easytoddlermeal

CARROT EGGLESS PANCAKES

We eat a lot of eggs for breakfast and I wanted to try a different protein source. I come up with most of my recipes by looking in my refrigerator and seeing what I need to use up. Buying a large bucket of yogurt because it's cheaper to buy in bulk backfires on me all the time. I can never finish it. On this particular day, the yogurt was about to expire.

Tip: Don't expect your traditional pancake texture; it's fluffier and creamier. The consistency is also a better, softer option for younger babies.

Prep Time: 10 minutes
Cooking Time: 5 minutes
Total Time: 15 minutes
Yield: 1-2 servings

Ingredients:

- 1 ripe banana
- ⅓ cup all-purpose flour
- ½ tsp baking powder
- ⅓ cup plain yogurt (I'm sure you can use flavored if you wish, just expect to taste that flavor)
- ¼ cup grated carrots

Procedure:

1. In a bowl, mix plain yogurt and ripe bananas. Smash and combine well.
2. In another bowl, mix all-purpose flour with baking powder
3. Mix banana mixture with flour mixture and add grated carrots.
4. In a pan, add butter and pour batter into circles.
5. Flip when bubbles appear and sides are golden.

Tip: If you use more batter for each pancake, it will be thicker.

See video! on

BREAKFAST

EGG TOAST CUPS

I always feel like I'm playing catch up. I'm constantly running out the door to get to work or to my son's swim class. Having these in the freezer is very convenient. They're easy to pack and are quite nutritious. I've also used other fillings including my favorite tuna salad (recipe in the book) instead of eggs before. The video below shows two options, one with a sunny side up egg and another with scrambled eggs. I still prefer to give my toddler fully cooked eggs, so I gave him the scrambled.

Prep Time: 5 minutes
Cooking Time: 10 minutes
Total Time: 15 minutes
Yield: 2 servings

Ingredients:

- 4 slices of fresh bread
- 4 eggs
- seasoning of choice, we used 21 seasoning salute from trader joes
- chopped spinach (optional)
- shredded cheese
- olive oil (for muffin tin)

Procedure:

1. Preheat oven to 350°F
2. Use a bowl to mold out a circle shape. I use a pizza cutter to make it easier to shape. (See video). Remove ends.
3. Carefully place bread circles into a greased muffin pan. Push center inside each circle.
4. For a sunny side up egg, simply break an egg into the bread cup. If you have large eggs, some may spill over to the next circle, so use medium size. Bake at 350°F for about 10-12 minutes (depending on how cooked you like your egg).
5. For scrambled eggs, scrambled eggs in a pan. Fill the bread cup with the cooked eggs and top with cheese (optional). Bake at 350°F for about 5 minutes, or just enough time for the cheese to melt and the bread to be slightly toasted.

BREAKFAST

BLUEBERRY BITES

Ingredients:

- 1 cup quick oats
- 2 large ripe bananas (the riper the sweeter it will be, we like them just right)
- ⅓ cup fresh blueberries

Procedure:

1. Preheat oven to 350°F
2. Mash bananas and add oats. Combine well.
3. Mix blueberries in with bananas and oats
4. Grease a baking sheet
5. Use an ice cream scooper or spoon to scoop mixture and place on a greased baking sheet
6. Bake at 350°F for 12-15 minutes

My son disliked bananas for the longest time. While this recipe essentially hides the banana, I always offer any food in its natural state before hiding it. If I hide a banana in a recipe for example, I will offer that dish and then a banana right next to it. After continuous trying, he has learned to love it and now asks for it. So don't give up!

These are great for breakfast or as a snack.

Prep Time: 5 minutes
Cooking Time: 15 minutes
Total Time: 20 minutes
Yield: 12 Bites

BREAKFAST

CHEESE SPINACH MUFFINS

This is my all-time favorite muffin because it contains almost all of the major food groups. If you're like most parents, some days you just don't want to cook more than one dish to satisfy the food pyramid. It's a big bonus that these muffins are nutritious and tasty.

I've found the best way to freeze these muffins is to wrap them in tin foil, place them in a ziplock bag, and store them in the freezer for later. Defrost the muffins by placing them in the refrigerator overnight. Heat it in the microwave for a few seconds when ready to eat.

Prep Time: 10 minutes
Cooking Time: 20 minutes
Total Time: 30 minutes
Yield: 12 Muffins

Ingredients:

- 1.5 cups of flour
- 1.5 tbs sugar
- 1 tbs baking powder
- ½ tsp salt
- 3 cups grated cheddar cheese
- 1 cup milk
- 1 cup chopped spinach
- 1 egg
- ½ stick of melted unsalted butter (4 tbs)

Procedure:

1. Preheat oven to 375ºF
2. Mix flour, sugar, baking powder, salt, chopped spinach and cheese in bowl
3. Mix milk, egg, and melted butter in another bowl
4. Combine flour mixture with milk mixture (dry and wet)
5. Pour mixture into a greased muffin pan
6. Bake at 375ºF for 20-25 minutes or until a toothpick comes out clean

BREAKFAST

THE PATTERNED SANDWICHES

Ingredients:

- cream cheese
- cucumber
- white bread
- strawberries

Procedure:

1. Use a peeler to cut very thin slices of cucumber and strawberries. You can also use a knife.
2. Heat cream cheese in the microwave for 15 seconds (just to soften it up). You can also just use spreadable cream cheese.
3. Spread cream cheese on bread
4. Layer cucumber, with some parts overlapping. Cut off bread ends.
5. Repeat same steps above for strawberries

Every time I make a cucumber and cream cheese sandwich, the cucumber falls off. To fix that problem I came up with these little sandwiches. They just so happen to be beautiful. If you know me personally, I love creating party decor and food. I'll definitely make these the next time I throw a shower or a birthday party. They're easy, affordable, and also appealing to the eye!

Prep Time: 10 minutes
Cooking Time: None
Total Time: 10 minutes
Yield: Varies

BREAKFAST

BREAKFAST BITES TO-GO

This is great for busy days, especially when you need to grab breakfast on the go. It also has an added vegetable in it and freezes well. Be sure you cook the yolk through for younger children.

Prep Time: 15 minutes
Cooking Time: 20 minutes
Total Time: 35 minutes
Yield: 4 Bites

Ingredients:

- four large eggs
- 1 sweet potato
- 21 seasonings salute (trader joes, or any seasonings you want)
- 2 strips of organic turkey bacon (cooked in a skillet for a few, but still flexible
- ½ cup shredded mozzarella cheese, or italian blend

Procedure:

1. Preheat oven to 350ºF
2. Peel and cut up sweet potato into match sticks or skinny fries
3. Grease muffin tin with olive oil spray
4. Add sweet potato in each muffin circle then add a ittle more olive oil spray
5. Add cheese on top of the sweet potato and carve a little hole in the middle for the egg
6. Crack a whole egg into one muffin circle (check video below)
7. Add cooked turkey bacon on top and seasonings
8. Bake at 350ºF for about 20-25 minutes; check it at about 20 min

BREAKFAST

QUINOA OATMEAL

Jazz up your oatmeal with more protein. Add quinoa to your everyday breakfast dish.

Prep Time: 5 minutes
Cooking Time: 8 hours
Total Time: 8 hours, 5 minutes
Yield: 2-3 Servings

Ingredients:

- 1 cup old fashioned oats
- ½ cup quinoa rinse well
- 4 ½ cups of water
- fruit for toppings
- honey

Procedure:

1. In a pot, add water and bring to a boil
2. Add all ingredients except fruit and honey
3. Simmer for 3 minutes, stirring occasionally
4. Remove from heat, cover and allow to cool
5. Place covered pot in fridge for at least 8 hours
6. Reheat when ready to serve and top with toppings and honey

Note: No honey before one years of age

BREAKFAST

STRAWBERRY CREAM CHEESE ROLLUPS

This is my go-to breakfast. Not only is it delicious, it's easy to grasp for kids. I personally can eat way too many of these for my own good. Fortunately, my toddler doesn't ever leave too many behind. Instead of a sugar coating, we use 100% organic applesauce for dipping.

Prep Time: 5 minutes
Cooking Time: 5 minutes
Total Time: 10 minutes
Yield: 5 rollups

Ingredients:

- 5 slices bread
- 3 tbs cream cheese (room temp or spreadable)
- 1 egg
- 1 tbs milk or milk of choice
- strawberries, chopped
- 2 tbs butter

Procedure:

1. Flatten bread with rolling pin or glass and remove crusts with a knife or pizza cutter.
2. Spread cream cheese on one side of the bread
3. Add chopped strawberries to bread, making sure not to over stuff
4. Carefully roll the bread and set aside. Repeat same steps above for all bread slices
5. In a bowl whisk egg and milk
6. Dip bread rolls into milk mixture
7. Cook in a pan with butter. Flip and cook each side evenly until brown

Serve with applesauce or plain

BREAKFAST

PIZZA BITES

Curb your pizza craving with this healthier option. Try making a pizza with sandwich bread; it's fast, easy, simple and delicious. You can choose what kind of bread you like to make it more nutritious. It's not dough, but at least you can eat just one and not feel too guilty about it.

Prep Time: 5 minutes
Cooking Time: 5 minutes
Total Time: 10 minutes
Yield: 2 pizza bites

Ingredients:

- 2 slices sandwich bread of choice
- ¼ cup white shredded cheddar cheese
- 2 chopped sweet bell peppers
- pizza sauce

Procedure:

1. Preheat oven to 375ºF
2. Use a glass or a small bowl to mold out a circle from a square sandwich (use a pizza cutter for easier trimming)
3. Spread pizza sauce on bread
4. Add cheese, then top with sweet bell peppers
5. Bake at 375ºF until toasted

LUNCH

BLOOMING SPINACH

This recipe is great as an appetizer for parties or a side dish for a meal. We had it with some tomato chicken.

You can reduce the garlic or spinach if you'd like.

Prep Time: 10 minutes
Cooking Time: 25 minutes
Total Time: 35 minutes
Yield: 4 servings

Ingredients:

- 1 unsliced sourdough bread round
- ¼ cup chopped spinach
- 1 tbs garlic
- 8 tbs melted butter
- 10 oz sliced cheddar cheese

Procedure:

1. Preheat oven to 350 °F
2. Using a knife, cut sourdough bread in squares (see video on site). Start cutting lines lengthwise, then widthwise through the crust, but not all the way through.
3. In a bowl, mix melted butter, garlic, and chopped spinach. Set aside
4. Fill each cut with cheese.
5. Pour butter mixture on top of the bread.
6. Place foil on baking sheet. Use another piece of foil to cover bread. Bake covered at 350ºF for 15 minutes.
7. Uncover, and bake again for about 6-7 minutes or until cheese melts.

LUNCH

KALE PASTA SALAD

This pasta salad is great for potlucks and is sure to be a hit. I reduced the amount of dressing for my toddler because of the sodium.

I've packed this dish in ball mason jars (pictured). It's the perfect size for portion control, although it did make me want more.

Prep Time: 5 minutes
Cooking Time: 15 minutes
Total Time: 20 minutes
Yield: 8-10 servings

Ingredients:

- 16 oz box rotini spiral pasta
- 1 cup newman's own creamy balsamic dressing / to taste if you want less
- 2 tbs agave nectar or honey (no honey before one)
- juice of one whole lemon
- kale salad or fresh uncooked broccoli
- salt and pepper to taste

Procedure:

1. Cook pasta per box directions.
2. Drain and cool
3. Mix all ingredients together

LUNCH

BROCCOLI CHEESE ROLL-UPS

Ingredients:

- sandwich bread (white fresh bread works best, stale bread cracks)
- steamed broccoli florets
- shredded or block cheese
- 3 tbs melted butter
- 2 tbs regular butter
- glass or rolling pin

Procedure:

1. Cut corners of bread
2. Flatten bread with a glass or rolling pin
3. Add cheese and broccoli to top of bread
4. Roll neatly and tightly
5. Dip in melted butter
6. Add butter to a pan and brown rolled sandwich

Tip: You can use just about any filling. Here are some examples:
- Peanut butter and jelly
- Strawberry and cream cheese
- Egg, avocado and cheese

Some of you may have found me from reading about my popular Stuffed French Toast recipe (included in this book).

I wanted to change it up to see if I can make it without egg. After creating this recipe, I am conflicted over which one is better because both are equally delicious! This recipe is very flexible; the amounts listed are at your discretion depending on what ingredient you like most. The more you stuff it, the bigger your roll-up will be.

Be careful though, if you stuff it too much, it may not close! You can always use a toothpick though (not advisable for younger babies of course).

Prep Time: 10 minutes
Cooking Time: 5 minutes
Total Time: 15 minutes
Yield: Varies

LUNCH

29

TUNA CRANBERRY ALMOND SALAD SANDWICH CIRCLES

Ingredients:

- bread
- 1 can wild caught tuna
- ¼ cup cranberries (try to find the lowest sugar level for baby)
- ¼ cup sliced or chopped almonds
- 2 tbs chopped green onions
- 2 tbs mayonnaise
- dash of pepper

Procedure:

1. Mix all ingredients
2. Top bread with tuna

We try to avoid canned food, but when we do use it, we kick it up a notch. I'm sharing my absolute favorite recipe for tuna sandwiches. When I was in college, this was my go-to, quick meal during those late night study sessions. Fast forward more years than I care to share, here I am making it for my two boys (husband and son).

As I may have mentioned previously, my son loves anything bite size. He ate about 10 of these tasty little morsels the first time I made them! I didn't have a small cookie cutter, so I used an old, clean baby bottle; it's better than throwing it away right? You can also use a Starbucks glass bottle or anything circular.

Feel free to adjust the quantities of individual ingredients to suit your tastes. This is also delicious if you substitute the mayo with avocado.

Prep Time: 5 minutes
Cooking Time: None
Total Time: 5 minutes
Yield: Varies

LUNCH

See video! on

STUFFED FRENCH TOAST

The best thing about this dish is you can stuff it with just about anything. Seriously, the possibilities are endless. Strawberry and cream cheese, peanut butter and jelly, butter and jam, apples and cinnamon, and so on and so on.

Prep Time: 5 minutes
Cooking Time: 5 minutes
Total Time: 10 minutes
Yield: 2 rollups

Ingredients:

- 2 slices of bread
- ½ avocado
- mozzarella shredded cheese
- 1 egg
- 1 tbs milk
- butter for cooking

Tip: You can always just use butter on both sides instead of milk and egg. Cut in strips for beginners.

Procedure:

1. Spread avocado on one side of bread
2. Add cheese
3. Place second piece of bread on top of first piece of bread. Cut in desired slices
4. In a bowl, whisk milk and egg
5. Dip bread into egg mixture and cook in butter in a pan

LUNCH

CAULIFLOWER MOZZARRELLA STICKS

It's so good; I'll make it short and sweet and get right to the point.

Prep Time: 10 minutes
Cooking Time: 25 minutes
Total Time: 35 minutes
Yield: 6-8 mozzarella sticks

Ingredients:

- 1 ½ cups cups of raw cauliflower
- ⅔ cup breadcrumbs
- 21 seasoning salute to taste (if you don't have this you can put some garlic or onion powder instead to taste)
- 2 string cheese
- 1 egg
- 2 tbs olive oil for frying

Procedure:

1. Steam cauliflower
2. Blend cauliflower, egg, breadcrumbs, and seasoning - until pasty. If your mixture is too sticky, add more breadcrumbs
3. Cut string cheese into ½ inch pieces, I've tried longer pieces, but they tend to fall apart.
4. Use an ice cream scoop and place on your wet hand
5. Add string cheese in the middle and cover it with the mixture (see video)
6. Add olive oil to pan and cook until brown

LUNCH

MACADAMIA CRUSTED COD
WITH MANGO SALSA

I first tried this dish in Hawaii. Since vacations come few and far between these days, I decided to bring the islands to my house instead. So delicious and relatively easy to make!

Prep Time: 5 minutes
Cooking Time: 20 minutes
Total Time: 25 minutes
Yield: 2 servings

Ingredients for Fish:

- 2 frozen cod fillets
- 2 tbs olive oil
- salt and pepper to taste
- 2 tbs mayonnaise
- ¼ cup of crushed macadamia nuts

Procedure:

1. Preheat oven to 450ºF
2. On a baking sheet, brush olive oil on both sides of the fillet, salt and pepper to taste
3. Bake for about 4-5 Minutes
4. Carefully remove the baking sheet from the oven (it will be hot!).
5. Spread mayonnaise on each fillet
6. Top with macadamia nuts and bake for another 15 minutes at 350ºF. Please check frequently or use an internal digital temperature and until it reaches 135ºF

Ingredients for Salsa:

- 1 mango, chopped in squares
- ⅛ cup red onion chopped (you can add more if you like onions)
- juice of ½ a lime

Procedure:

1. Chop all ingredients and mix

DINNER

CREAMY MUSHROOM CHICKEN

This dish is so creamy and rich. It takes only 5 minutes of prep time and is baked in the oven.

Prep Time: 5 minutes
Cooking Time: 30 minutes
Total Time: 35 minutes
Yield: 2 Servings

Ingredients:

- 4 boneless chicken thighs, breast will work too
- 1 tbs minced garlic
- 1 tsp salt (to taste, but I think this depends on your soup and how salty it already is)
- 1 can cream of mushroom condensed soup
- ½ cup of shredded parmesan cheese
- ½ cup heavy cream, add more if you feel the soup is too condensed
- ½ cup of fresh mushrooms
- parsley for garnish

Procedure:

1. Preheat oven to 365ºF
2. Combine garlic, salt, and shredded cheese in a bowl
3. Add chicken into a baking dish.
4. Top chicken with garlic mixture (#2)
5. In another bowl mix cream of mushroom and heavy cream, pour evenly over the chicken making sure each piece is covered with cream.
6. Bake at 365ºF until internal temperature reaches 165ºF. Again, I always use a leave in thermometer to prevent overcooking, took about an hour though.

DINNER

SWEET AND SOUR CHICKEN MEATBALLS

I grew up eating Asian food every day so naturally, I am often more inclined to make Asian dishes for my own family. Here is a great alternative to your standard, round-the-corner, Chinese take-out, sweet and sour dish. The meatballs without the sauce are great to eat too. Plus, it's a great "hide-the-veggies" dish!

Prep Time: 15 minutes
Cooking Time: 25 minutes
Total Time: 40 minutes
Yield: 4 servings

Ingredients for Meatball:

- 1 lb ground chicken
- 1 grated sweet apple
- ½ grated pear (optional)
- 1 lightly beaten egg
- ½ tsp salt
- ½ tsp pepper
- 1 tsp dijon mustard
- ¼ cup chopped spinach
- 1 cup panko breadcrumbs / quinoa if you want to go glutenfree
- ⅓ cup chopped green onion (if you like less onion then reduce)

Ingredients for Sweet and Sour Sauce:

- 2 tbs water
- 2 tbs ketchup
- ½ cup brown sugar
- 1 tbs corn starch
- ⅓ cup rice vinegar, add more if you like it more sour

Procedure for Meatball:

1. Preheat oven to 350ºF
2. Mix all ingredients in a bowl
3. Shape and mold. I use an ice cream scooper.
4. Bake at 350ºF until internal temperature 165ºF. It usually takes about 20-25 minutes, but it really depends on the oven. Use an internal meat thermometer.

Procedure for Sauce:

1. Add all ingredients except for the corn starch and water into a pot, wait for a boil
2. Mix water and cornstarch in a bowl
3. Add into boiling mixture and whisk
4. Pour sauce over meatballs and serve with rice or noodle

DINNER

SLOW COOKER BEEF AND BROCCOLI

I usually make this dish in a wok, but I was extremely busy with work one day so I threw it all in a slow cooker instead. Lo and behold it worked out beautifully and is one of my go-to dishes.

Prep Time: 5 minutes
Cooking Time: 6 hours
Total Time: 6 hours, 5 minutes
Yield: 4 servings

Ingredients:

- ½ cup low sodium soy sauce
- ⅓ cup brown sugar
- 2 tbs sesame oil
- 3 cloves garlic (chopped)
- 1 cup low sodium beef broth
- 1 lb stir fry cut beef
- 1 red bell pepper (chopped)
- 2 large broccoli stalks
- dash of pepper

Procedure:

1. In a bowl, whisk soy sauce, sugar, sesame oil, garlic, beef broth and pepper
2. Add beef to mixture and place in in slow cooker on low until tender (usually 4-6 hours depending on cooker)
3. Add broccoli and red pepper 30 minutes before serving, unless you like soggy veggies
4. Serve over white rice

DINNER

BELL PEPPER BEEF STEAK

This dish is inspired by my Filipino roots. It's such an easy recipe and so delicious. I always strive to instill culture in our family and one way I do that is through my cooking.

You can do without all the bell pepper varieties if you wish.

Prep Time: 30 minutes
Cooking Time: 10 minutes
Total Time: 40 minutes
Yield: 4 servings

Ingredients:

- 1 lb top sirloin beef
- ¼ red bell pepper (cut in strips)
- ¼ orange red bell pepper (cut in strips)
- ¼ yellow red bell pepper (cut in strips)
- ¼ red onion (cut in rings)
- ¼ cup tamari or low sodium soy sauce
- ½ tsp garlic
- 1 tsp corn starch
- ¼ tsp black pepper
- juice of ¼ of a lemon
- 2 tbs olive oil

Procedure:

1. Cut sirloin beef to thin slices
2. Whisk soy sauce, garlic, cornstarch, pepper, and lemon juice in a bowl
3. Add beef to mixture
4. Marinate for at least 30 minutes in the refrigerator
5. In a pan, heat 1 tbs olive oil and sauté onions and bell peppers. Set aside.
6. In the same pan, heat another 1 tbs olive oil and brown beef on medium high, until cooked
7. Top with veggies and serve over rice

DINNER

BAKED CHICKEN PARMESAN WITH "NOODLES"

This dish is a marriage between two worlds, pasta and veggie. It includes a spiralized zucchini mixed in with spaghetti, and also chopped spinach on top. The chicken parmesan makes it even tastier.

Prep Time: 10 minutes
Cooking Time: 20 minutes
Total Time: 30 minutes
Yield: 4 servings

Ingredients:

- 4 chicken breasts (cut in half to make 8)
- 1 cups breadcrumbs
- ½ cups grated parmesan cheese
- 1 tsp paprika (reduce if you like)
- ¼ tsp italian seasoning
- 1 zucchini
- ½ pound spaghetti
- 1 cups marinara sauce (home made or store bought)
- ½ cups shredded mozzarella cheese
- 2 tbs olive oil
- olive oil spray

Procedure:

1. Preheat oven to 450ºF
2. In a bowl, mix breadcrumbs, parmesan cheese, paprika, and italian seasoning
3. Cut chicken breasts in half to make thinner slices
4. Brush olive oil on each chicken breast on both sides
5. Dip chicken breast in bread crumbs mixture until fully coated
6. Spray cooking oil on a baking sheet and add to place coated chicken breast on sheet. Spray a little oil on top.
7. Bake for about 15- 20 minutes, then flip over for another 5 minutes
8. Top with marinara sauce and mozzarella cheese and bake again for 1 minute until cheese melts.
9. Spiralize zucchini (I use Spiralizer) and cook spaghetti per box directions
10. Combine zucchini and spaghetti (You can also saute the zucchini in a little butter if desired for a few minutes).
11. Serve chicken on top of combination zoodles and spaghetti. Mix in marinara sauce in pasta and add chopped spinach (optional)

DINNER

CHILI CORNBREAD MUFFINS

My husband absolutely loves chili. No offense to canned chili lovers, but I don't particularly love the ingredients in it. This was an experiment in the kitchen since my specialty is usually Asian food. I asked my husband what the main ingredients were and went for it! When I was through, my husband said, "You can definitely cook this again, it's delicious."

If you're wondering how I came up with the chili muffin idea; my toddler inspired me. Like always, I try to find ways to make it an easier eating experience for both baby and me. Adding some chili in the middle made it simpler for our son to eat and makes for a much easier cleanup.

Prep Time: 10 minutes
Cooking Time: 4-6 hours
Total Time: 6 hours, 10 minutes
Yield: 12 muffins

Ingredients for Chili:

- 1 lb ground beef
- 2 - 8 oz cans of tomato sauce
- 1 tbs chopped garlic
- 1 can black beans or kidney beans
- 1 tbs chili powder (you can do two, but I didn't want it too spicy for baby)
- 1 tbs sugar
- ¼ cup water
- 1 tsp cumin powder
- seasoning salt to taste
- 1 tbs olive oil (for browning)

Chili procedure:

1. In a pan heat olive oil. Add ground beef until brown Add a little seasoning salt to beef
2. Add all the ingredients into the slow cooker. I only put a dash of salt and pepper because of the baby, but you can always add more to taste.
3. Slow cook for 4-6 hours on low

Ingredients for Cornbread Muffins:

- 1 cup all-purpose flour
- 1 cup buttermilk
- 1 cup cornmeal
- ½ tsp salt
- ½ tsp baking soda
- 2 eggs
- ⅓ cup white sugar
- 1 stick unsalted butter (½ cup)
- 1 tsp sour cream

Cornbread procedure:

1. Preheat oven to 375ºF
2. Melt butter in microwave and stir in sugar in bowl #1
3. Add eggs to bowl #1 and beat well
4. In another bowl (#2) mix buttermilk and baking soda
5. Add buttermilk mixture (#2) to bowl #1 and add sour cream
6. Mix well and pour into muffin tin pan. Optional to use muffin liner cups. If you don't, make sure you grease your pan.
7. Bake for about 15-20 minutes, until a toothpick inserted in the center comes out clean

DINNER

ONE PAN CHICKEN TENDERS WITH ASPARAGUS

I call these grown up chicken nuggets. A mom and dad can only eat so many chicken nuggets right? It takes just a few minutes to prepare and about half an hour to bake.

Prep Time: 5 minutes
Cooking Time: 30 minutes
Total Time: 35 minutes
Yield: 4 servings

Ingredients:

- 1 pound chicken breast tenders
- ¼ cup breadcrumbs
- ½ cup shredded parmesan cheese
- 1 tbs organic ranch powder mix
- salt and pepper to taste
- one bunch of asparagus
- 4 tbs butter, melted or olive oil

Procedure:

1. Preheat oven to 350ºF
2. In a bowl, mix breadcrumbs, parmesan cheese, and ranch
3. Salt and pepper chicken breast tenders if desired. Keep in mind the cheese and ranch already have some salt (depending on brand)
4. In another bowl, pour melted butter or olive oil
5. Dip chicken tender one by one in melted butter/olive oil (both sides)
6. Roll chicken tender in breadcrumb mixture
7. Brush olive oil on asparagus
8. Grease a baking pan with olive oil and add chicken tenders and asparagus
9. Bake for about 30-40 minutes (depends on oven) or until internal temperature is 165ºF

Tip: Use an internal thermometer to prevent dry chicken.

DINNER

FROZEN BANANAS

A tasty summer treat that's also fun for the kids to make.

Prep Time: 5 minutes
Cooking Time: 3 hours
Total Time: 3 hours, 5 minutes
Yield: Varies

Ingredients:

- bananas
- greek yogurt
- toppings of choice - crushed walnuts, almonds, coconut, or pomegranate
- popsicle sticks

Procedure:

1. Cut bananas in half
2. Insert popsicle stick ¾ through banana
3. Pour some greek yogurt on a plate
4. Roll banana in greek yogurt
5. Roll banana in toppings
6. Freeze for at least 3 hours and serve

DESSERT

GREEN CHOCOLATE CHIP COOKIES

My son got hurt the day I made these. I used a bag of frozen peas to place on his bruise. I forgot about them and an hour later I realized I had to use them. I added them to chocolate chip cookies and they were delicious. Sounds like an odd combination, but they tasted great. Don't turn your nose to it until you try it!

It also has no added sugar. You can switch to cacao nibs if you're concerned about the refined sugar in chocolate chips. In my humble opinion, however, a chocolate chip cookie isn't a chocolate chip cookie without chocolate chips.

Prep Time:	10 minutes
Cooking Time:	10 minutes
Total Time:	20 minutes
Yield:	24 cookies

Ingredients:

- 2 ripe bananas
- 1 cup melted butter
- ¼ cup green peas
- 1 egg
- 2 ¼ cup flour
- ½ tsp salt
- 1 tsp baking soda
- 1 tsp vanilla
- 1 cup chocolate chips

Procedure:

1. Preheat oven to 375ºF
2. In a blender, blend peas, bananas, and egg. Set aside.
3. In a bowl, combine flour and mixed peas mixture.
4. Add melted butter, baking soda, vanilla and chocolate chips and stir
5. Use an ice cream scooper and place on an ungreased cookie sheet. Bake for about 8-10 minutes or until a toothpick comes out clean

DESSERT

CINNAMON TOAST STICKS

We try to be a no-waste household whenever possible. Several of my recipes involve removing the bread crusts and admittedly, I too love sandwiches without the crust. After I remove the crusts, I save them in a zip lock bag and use them to make these cinnamon sticks. So don't throw out those scraps, and try this dish! Trust me you'll feel better, but then perhaps a little worse after you've consumed about 80 of these.

Prep Time: 5 minutes
Cooking Time: 5 minutes
Total Time: 10 minutes
Yield: 3 servings

Ingredients:

- 4 cups sandwich bread crusts
- 3 tbs melted butter
- 1 tbs brown sugar (you can add more, but I wanted to keep it somewhat healthy)
- 1 tsp cinnamon

Procedure:

1. Preheat oven to 350ºF
2. In a bowl, drizzle melted butter on the sandwich bread crusts. Mix well so each piece gets butter on it.
3. Mix in brown sugar and cinnamon
4. Bake at 350ºF for 6-8 minutes

Tip: You can also make garlic parmesan sticks; just replace sugar and cinnamon with parmesan cheese and fresh chopped garlic.

DESSERT

FRENCH TOAST STICKS

While similar to their cinnamon toast stick cousins, French toast sticks are decidedly different, but equally delicious It's especially great because kids can easily grasp it.

Prep Time: 5 minutes
Cooking Time: 5 minutes
Total Time: 10 minutes
Yield: Varies

Ingredients:

- bread crusts
- 1 egg
- 3 tbs milk
- 2 tbs butter

Procedure:

1. Whisk milk and egg
2. Dip bread crusts in egg mixture
3. In a pan, cook bread crusts in butter.

Serve with applesauce or pear puree

DESSERT

BANANA WALNUT ICE CREAM
WITH BUTTERY BANANAS

Who doesn't like ice cream? I personally can eat a whole pint in one sitting if I let myself. One of my favorite flavors is banana walnut, but I can rarely find it anywhere outside of an ice cream specialty store. Hence my craving for the hard to find paved the way for this creamy goodness. It's baby friendly, just omit the honey for children under one years of age.

Prep Time: 5 minutes
Cooking Time: 2 hours
Total Time: 2 hours, 5 minutes
Yield: 2 Servings

Ingredients:

- 2 bananas
- ½ cup of heavy cream
- ¼ cup walnuts
- honey (no honey before one, you can substitute it with maple syrup or omit all together)

Procedure for Ice Cream:

1. Blend all ingredients except honey, unless you want it
2. Freeze for about an hour to an hour and half. Any longer and it will be too frozen. You can also let it defrost a bit, before eating.

Just remember it won't have the same consistency as store-bought ice cream, but it's pretty close. You can also top it off with more walnuts and honey!

Ingredients for Banana Topping:

- one banana (cut)
- honey
- 2 tbs butter

Procedure for Toppings:

1. Cook in butter until brown. Then add honey.
2. Serve on top of ice cream

DESSERT

APPLE CHOCOLATE CHIPS

I love cutting up apples thinly like chips. Why not add some chocolate and almonds on it? I used raw cacao, but regular melted chocolate is a great option to use. You can also poke a lollipop stick in it for a great treat at birthday parties.

Prep Time: 5 minutes
Cooking Time: 1 hour
Total Time: 1 hour, 5 minutes
Yield: Varies

Ingredients:

- 1-2 tbs agave syrup (we used 1, if you like it sweeter, make it 2)
- ⅓ cup raw cacao powder
- 3 tbs of coconut oil
- apples, strawberries, or fruit of choice
- toppings: crushed almond and shredded coconut

Procedure:

1. Mix agave sugar, cacao powder in a bowl
2. In a pan heat coconut oil until liquid form (this will take a few seconds, don't burn it)
3. Mix 1 and 2 together
4. Dip fruit in chocolate mixture and let it drip until it stops
5. Place dipped fruit on parchment paper and place in refrigerator for at least an hour

Thank me. Kidding.

DESSERT

BANANA CARROT LOAVES

Did you know antioxidant levels increase as a banana ages? Problem is, I can't stand eating them, when they're overripe. Naturally, I decided to make banana bread. I changed it up a bit by making mini loaves with a twist. If you want a sweeter loaf you can add ⅓ cup of sugar. We love it without!

On a side note, you can wrap these loaves in cute wrapping paper for cute party favors! If you want to know what else I do for fun, check out my "things I do at midnight" on my blog.

Prep Time: 10 minutes
Cooking Time: 15 minutes
Total Time: 25 minutes
Yield: 10 mini loaves

Ingredients:

- ½ cups grated carrots
- 3 ripe bananas
- 1 egg
- 3 tbs. coconut oil
- 2 tsp. vanilla extract
- ¼ cups greek yogurt
- 1 ½ cups flour
- 1 tsp. baking powder
- ½ tsp. baking soda
- ½ tsp. salt

Procedure:

1. Preheat oven to 350ºF
2. Blend first 5 ingredients in a blender. If you want the carrots to be intact, exclude it from the blend and add after.
3. In a bowl, mix all dry ingredients
4. Combine wet and dry ingredients
5. Bake at 350ºF for about 16-17 minutes. Check at 15 min with a toothpick. If it comes out clean, it's ready.

DESSERT

VEGGIE "CUPCAKES" WITH GREEK YOGURT FROSTING

This is a new twist to on an old favorite recipe. I decided to add a few variations and I also topped it off with a slightly healthier frosting/spread. You can make it a "no refined sugar" recipe by omitting the sugar and/or frosting; it tastes great either way.

Prep Time: 10 minutes
Cooking Time: 15 minutes
Total Time: 25 minutes
Yield: 12 cupcakes

Wet ingredients:

- ½ cup unsweetened applesauce
- 1 cup spinach
- 1 ripe banana
- 1 large grated yellow squash (I've used 1 carrot as well)
- ¼ cup raw cashews (optional)
- 1 egg
- 2 tbs sugar (optional)
- 2.5 tbs coconut oil
- 2 tsp vanilla extract

Dry ingredients:

- 1 tsp baking powder
- ½ tsp baking soda
- ½ tsp salt
- 1.5 cups of all-purpose flour

Procedure for Cupcakes:

1. Preheat oven to 350ºF
2. Blend wet ingredients until mixed well.
3. Mix dry ingredients in a bowl
4. Combine wet ingredients with dry ingredients
5. Grease muffin tin
6. Pour into muffin tin (leave some room for rising),
7. Bake at 350ºF for about 16-17 minutes, check at 15 minutes with a toothpick. If it comes out clean it's done.

Ingredients for Greek Yogurt Spread:

- 2 oz cream cheese (softened)
- 2.5 tbs greek yogurt
- 1 tbs powdered sugar

Procedure for Spread:

1. Beat together cream cheese and greek yogurt until smooth. Sift in powder sugar. Add more sugar if you like it sweeter.

DESSERT

Made in the USA
Middletown, DE
31 July 2016